THE MINIATURE BOOK OF

Dried Flowers

MARY LAWRENCE

CRESCENT BOOKS
New York

This 1991 edition published by Crescent Books, distributed
by Outlet Book Company, Inc., a Random House Company,
225 Park Avenue South, New York, New York 10003, U.S.A.

© Salamander Books Ltd., 1991
129-137 York Way, London N7 9LG, United Kingdom

Printed and bound in Singapore

ISBN 0-517-03393-3
8 7 6 5 4 3 2

CREDITS

MANAGING EDITOR: *Jilly Glassborow*
EDITED BY: *Veronica Ross*
PHOTOGRAPHY BY: *Richard Paines*
DESIGN AND ARTWORK BY: *Pauline Bayne*
TYPESET BY: *SX Composing Ltd.*
COLOR SEPARATION BY: *P&W Graphics, Pte. Ltd.*
Printed in Singapore by Star Standard Industries Pte. Ltd.

CONTENTS

INTRODUCTION

In recent years the popularity of dried flowers has soared, and now all manner of stunning dried blooms are available. The finished displays are packed with colour, and can last for years. Mixed bunches of flowers can now be purchased in department stores, florists, and specialist shops, although the cheapest way of pursuing this hobby is to dry your own blooms.

There are several ways of drying flowers but air drying is probably the easiest. Bind the flowers into bunches and leave them hanging upside down in a warm, dark place for one to four weeks, depending on the type of plant. Specialist drying agents are also available. One of the easiest to use is silica gel which comes in the form of white crystals. Place a layer of crystals into the base of an airtight box and place the wired flowerheads on top. Using a spoon, carefully cover the flowers with crystals. Close the container and leave for a couple of days.

You will need to purchase some basic equipment before starting, such as dry foam to support your arrangement and various types of wire. Stub wires are straight lengths

of wire used for supporting single flower heads or binding plants together into small bunches. Reel wire is used for wreaths where a continuous length of wire is needed, and finer silver wire is used for delicate work, for example binding posies. You may also need wire mesh and pinholders for support, florists' adhesive or fixative to secure the supports, and clear glue to stick individual flowers in place.

When planning your arrangement, choose flowers to harmonize with your room or to enhance the design of a favourite vase. Start by copying some of the designs in this book until you feel confident enough to try out your own ideas and create your own original arrangements.

$\mathcal{S}$ILVER POSY

∾

12 stems lily of the valley
15 stems muscari & 9 cornflowers
5 pansies & 3 astrantia
7 narcissi & 2 stems pulmonaria
3 stems spurge
Salad burnett leaves (burnet)
Florists' stub wire
Silica gel & plastic box with lid
Silver bowl

This pretty miniature display has been carefully preserved in silica gel. Cut down the flower stems and push a stub wire into each stem. Pour an inch of silica gel crystals into a plastic box. Put the flowers in the box and gently sieve more crystals over them until the flowers are covered under a layer at least ½in (1cm) thick. Seal and leave for 2 or 3 days. Lift the flowers out carefully, and remove the crystals with a paint brush. Fill the bowl with crushed wire mesh, and gently insert the wired flowers to build up a posy shape. Use dried foliage to cover any visible wires.

$\mathcal{B}$LUE SKIES

∽

11 stems dried delphiniums
7 pink peonies
5 stems eucalyptus, (silver dollar tree – E. cinerea)
4 stems eucalyptus, (Tasmanian blue gum – E. globulus)
Wire mesh
Florists' adhesive tape
Glass vase

The design of this pale blue glass vase inspires and dictates the shape of this charming arrangement. The flowers follow the line of the vase, falling into a graceful shape. Cut a piece of wire mesh to fit over the top of the vase and secure in place with adhesive tape. Carefully position the delphiniums to follow their natural shape and fill in with the soft sprays of eucalyptus. Next, position the peonies to give depth to the design. Finally, arrange short stems of eucalyptus to spread over the front of the vase.

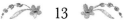

WALL FLOWERS

∾

6 peonies & 3 peonies in bud
1 bunch white larkspur
1 bunch pink larkspur
1 bunch deep pink helichrysum (strawflower or everlasting)
1 bunch pink broom blooms
1 bunch willow & myrtle
Shallow basket
Florists' dry foam & adhesive tape
Fast drying clear glue & stub wire
2 plastic pinholders & fixative

This wall display looks stunning arranged in a shallow basket. Thread wire through the top of the basket to make a hanger. Using green fixative, secure the plastic pinholders to one side of the base of the basket. Place foam onto the pinholder and secure with adhesive tape. Following the line of the basket, insert larkspur stems into the foam. Wire the other flowers into short bunches and fill in. Position peonies to form a central focal line and place the helichrysum below the peonies to create harmony and depth.

$\mathcal{V}$ICTORIAN POSY

7 pink roses
5 pink helichyrsum (strawflower or everlasting)
10 small poppy seed heads
1 bunch peach & 1 bunch bleached glixias
1 bunch bleached broom blooms
1 bunch glycerined male fern
Florists' silver reel wire
Florists' stub wire & stem tape
Cream lace & peach ribbon

$\mathcal{D}$ried flowers in various shades of pink and peach combine beautifully to make this wedding posy. Divide the broom blooms into short bunches and wire a stub wire to each bunch. Repeat with the glixias, and with each single flower and seed head. Cover the wires with tape. Start the posy by binding silver wire to a wired rose. Surround the rose with a circle of bleached glixias and bind in. Add a circle of roses, helichrysum and poppy heads, and a circle of broom. Twist the stub wires together to make a handle. Bind in a circle of peach and bleached glixias and fern. Decorate with ribbon and lace.

$\mathscr{S}$UMMER GLORY

12 burgundy-edged carnations
12 pink Japanese anemones
5 sprays spiraea
3 purple pom-pom dahlia
1 bunch purple & 1 bunch white statice
Dried moss
Florists' adhesive tape
Florists' reel wire, tape & stub wire
Cling film (plastic wrap)
Posy bowl

*T*his charming design has all the appeal of a fresh flower arrangement. To preserve your display and to retain the natural colours of the flowers, dry the individual blooms in silica gel before you start on your design (see page 11). Line the bowl with cling film then add a layer of moss. Cut foam to fit the bowl and secure to the bowl with adhesive tape. Start by building the shape with the statice and spiraea. Wire bunches of flowers together and work towards the edge of the posy bowl. Allow some of the blooms to curl over the rim.

$\mathcal{R}$USTIC CHARM

∾

7 peonies
3 globe artichoke heads
1 bunch of deep pink helichrysum (strawflower or everlasting)
1 bunch poppy seed heads
2 bunches helipterum & 1 bunch pink larkspur
1 bunch of oats & 1 bunch quaking grass
3 fern leaves & 3 sprays silver brunia
Rustic basket
Florists' dry foam & adhesive tape

The 'freshly gathered' look of this display is achieved by carefully selecting flowers and foliage to give an interesting outline and texture to the design. Secure the foam in the centre of the basket. Cut the ferns into three-inch (7cms) lengths and insert around the outside edge of the foam to create a 'collar'. Place a peony in the middle of the foam, just under the handle. Cut short bunches of smaller flowers and foliage and wire into groups. Turning the basket as you work, insert these around the edge. Build up the centre with bunches, individual flowers, artichoke and poppy heads.

HEARTH BASKET

7 pink roses
12 pinky/peach helichrysum (strawflower or everlasting)
1 bunch peach broom blooms
1 bunch dudinea
3 sprays peach anaphalis
Glycerined copper beech foliage
Lichen
Florists' dry foam & stub wires
Florists' adhesive tape
Log basket

During the summer months, use a log basket to display a charming arrangement of pink and beige flowers. Fill the basket with several blocks of dry foam. Level off with a sharp knife and secure with tape. Divide the lichen into flat pieces and pin into the foam to cover the basket. Wire the copper beech and fix to the basket to form a central 'S' shape. Following the outline, insert single wired roses and helichrysums. Wire broom, dudinea and anaphalis into small bunches and use to fill in.

LAVENDER BLUE

❧

1 bunch canary grass
2 bunches of lavender
2 blocks of florists' dry foam
Reel wire
Stem tape
Cling film (plastic wrap)
Fast drying clear glue
Flat backed wall basket

*I*nspired by Elizabethan garden engravings, this attractive wall design is built up by arranging alternate rows of lavender and canary grass. Fill the basket with foam and trim into a convex shape with a sharp knife. Cut down the canary grass stems to approximately one inch (2cms) and insert around the bottom edge of the basket. Next insert 4 rows of lavender, and keeping to the shape of the basket add further rows of canary grass. For a final decorative touch, wire together a few stems of lavender and grass into a small bunch and glue to the front of the basket.

$\mathscr{W}$ELCOME BASKET

∽

20 helichrysum (strawflower or everlasting)
20 pressed hydrangea florets
2 bunches sea lavender
Limonium latifolium/statice latifolia
Fragrant pot-pourri
1yd 1(m) paper ribbon
Plastic bag & black reel wire
Fast drying clear glue

his rustic wicker basket overflowing with colour makes a delightful display. Fill the basket with pot-pourri for a lasting fragrant arrangement. Using reel wire, bind short bundles of sea lavender to the basket handle, and also thread wired bunches of sea lavender to the rim of the basket. Cut a plastic bag to fit inside the basket and glue in place. Glue the hydrangea florets to the edge of the basket. Wait until the glue is dry and then glue the helichrysum heads into position. Loop paper ribbon around the handle and secure with a bow at both sides. Fill with your favourite pot-pourri mix.

$\mathcal{W}$OODLAND

3 bunches white larkspur
2 bunches green love-lies-bleeding
2 bunches broom blooms
2 bunches willow & myrtle
2 bunches immortelle (everlasting)
1 bunch helichrysum buds (strawflower or everlasting)
9 sprays floribunda roses
2 gnarled branches & shallow basket
Florists' foam & tape
Quick drying glue

$\mathcal{C}$reate an unusual indoor garden by using a colourful selection of dried flowers. Shape foam blocks to fit tightly into the basket and secure in position with tape. Insert the larkspur and love-lies-bleeding to stand 12ins (30cms) high at the centre back. Bank one side of the basket with myrtle. Glue the two gnarled branches in position across the centre. Cut down the immortelle and broom blooms and place in position. Insert a line of helichrysum vertically through the centre and a line of roses to cut across the design.

$\mathcal{A}$UTUMN BLAZE

❧

9 orange dyed protea
1 bunch glycerined eucalyptus
2 bunches glycerined wattle
1 bunch brown dyed quaking grass
Stems brown dyed grass
Reindeer moss
Florists' dry foam
Florists' reel wire & stub wire
Cling film (plastic wrap)
Basket

$\mathcal{C}$reate this dramatic, autumnal design by combining a selection of bronze coloured foliage and grasses with bright orange proteus. Line the basket with cling film. Pack tightly with foam and secure with tape. Cut stub wires and shape into 'hairpins'. Attach the pins to the reindeer moss and insert them into the foam to cover the surface. Arrange the foliage in a random shape to complement the shape of the basket and place the proteus to make points of interest. Wire the grasses into small bunches and use to fill in.

$\mathcal{E}$LIZABETHAN

1 bunch pink statice
1 bunch purple statice
1 bunch blue larkspur
1 bunch lime green broom, genista
1 bunch dark green broom
1 bunch green dyed African daisies
5 sprays of sea holly
Florists' reel wire & wire mesh
2 vases

A brilliantly coloured collection of dried flowers makes a striking display. Place a small posy of pink statice in the smaller jug to the foreground to cleverly balance the elements of the design. Fill the base of the large vase with crunched wire mesh. Position blue larkspur at the centre back. Unbunch the broom and carefully fan out until the bunch has doubled in size. Use the broom to build up the outline size. Fill in the shape with wired bunches of statice, larkspur and sea holly. Position the African daisies in the centre to complete.

$\mathcal{E}$DWARDIAN HAT

∽

5 orange dahlia
5 helichrysum (strawflower or everlasting)
Golden rod
12 ears of wheat
2 dryandra
Stems of quaking grass
Glycerined oak foliage
Moss
Florists' reel wire & stub wire
Glue & wreath wrap
Straw hat

$\mathcal{L}$iven up an old straw boater with a striking floral spray. Mould the moss into an egg shape and bind carefully with wire. Cover with wreath wrap and secure to the hat with reel wire threaded through the weave. Cut stems of wheat, wire them into clumps and push into the moss. Gradually wire in dahlias, helichrysum and oak leaves to form a bunch. Group the discarded stems into bunches and wire into the base of the arrangement. To finish, glue leaves around one side of the brim.

COPPER GLOW

∽

5 stems pampas grass
5 stems brown dyed oats
5 stems glycerined eucalyptus
3 stems Chinese lanterns
3 stems reedmace (small bullrush)
1 dried maize/corn head (Indian corn)
Copper kettle
Florists' foam & adhesive tape
Reel wire

The warm glow of an old copper kettle complements this autumnal display of dried grasses and flowers. Begin by wedging a block of dry foam into the kettle, allowing it to protude above the neck by 1½ins (4cms). Secure with adhesive tape. Use the foliage to make an outline shape then soften the line by positioning the pampas grass. Next, arrange the reedmace and Chinese lanterns into groups and position to cover the foam at the front. Lastly, pull back the bracts of the corn, cut the stem short and position to follow the line of the spout.

COTTAGE STYLE

∾

5 stems leucodendron
2 bunches peach helichrysum (strawflower or everlasting)
2 bunches nigella & 2 bunches sea lavender
2 bunches quaking grass
1 bunch peach dyed achillea
1 bunch peach dyed African daisies
1 bunch glycerined wattle (acacia)
Woven basket
Reel & stub wire
Florists' dry foam & adhesive tape
Cling film (plastic wrap)

*T*his delightful array of country flowers is designed to look like a freshly gathered display. Line the basket with cling film. Fill with foam and secure with tape. Cut down the stems of sea lavender and push into the foam to cover the surface. Position groups of flowers just above the height of the handle and around the perimeter of the basket. Wire flowers into mixed bunches and add to the basket. Insert brown wattle foliage to break up the solid look of the design.

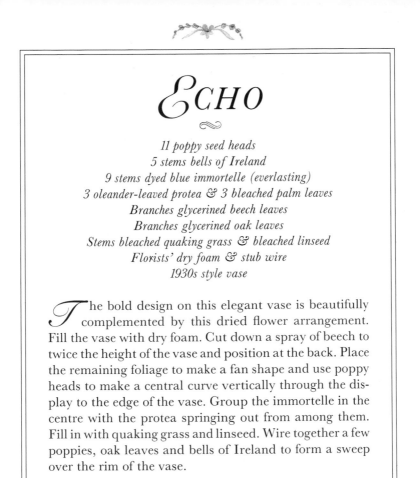

ℰCHO

11 poppy seed heads
5 stems bells of Ireland
9 stems dyed blue immortelle (everlasting)
3 oleander-leaved protea & 3 bleached palm leaves
Branches glycerined beech leaves
Branches glycerined oak leaves
Stems bleached quaking grass & bleached linseed
Florists' dry foam & stub wire
1930s style vase

The bold design on this elegant vase is beautifully complemented by this dried flower arrangement. Fill the vase with dry foam. Cut down a spray of beech to twice the height of the vase and position at the back. Place the remaining foliage to make a fan shape and use poppy heads to make a central curve vertically through the display to the edge of the vase. Group the immortelle in the centre with the protea springing out from among them. Fill in with quaking grass and linseed. Wire together a few poppies, oak leaves and bells of Ireland to form a sweep over the rim of the vase.

GOLDEN BLEND

∾

3 protea
3 open & 6 closed cones
1 maize/corn cob (Indian corn)
2 branches of hops
Ears of wheat
Strelitzia leaves (bird of paradise)
Eucalyptus & Chestnut leaves
Ferns
Florists dry foam
Plastic pinholder & fixative
Gold spray paint

*T*ransform the look of a dried flower arrangement by adding a touch of gold spray paint. This display would make a welcome addition to your sitting room. Place all the items in the lid of a large cardboard box and spray with gold paint. Make sure all the surfaces are covered. Secure dry foam into the container with fixative. Position strelitzia leaves and other foliage to form an 'L' shape. Group the cones and protea in the centre and allow the hops to spill over the edge of the container.

$\mathcal{F}$ESTIVE DISPLAY

3 white candles & 8 cones
2 vine wreaths, 9½ (24cms) and 12ins (30cms) diameter
3 artichokes & 1 bunch poppy seed heads
5 stems bupleurum & 3 stems buxifolium
1 bunch miniature everlasting & fern leaves
Rhododendron foliage & reindeer moss
Florists' 'staysoft' clay & round flat plate
Florists' stub wire, reel wire & adhesive tape
2yd (2m) red & 1yd (2m) tartan ribbon
Fire retardant spray & clear glue

This splendid Christmas design will last throughout
the holiday. Fix clay to the centre of the plate and
press in the candles. Place the large wreath over the plate
and build up foliage and bupleurum at the back, leaning
away from the candles. Add fern around the perimeter.
Insert poppy heads, cones and moss to one side of the
candles and make bows to fill the other side. Lean the
small wreath against the front of the large one, and fill the
centre with the remaining items. Finally, spray with fire
retardant spray.